This journal belongs to:

Partner A: _____

Partner B: _____

I do Solemnly Swear to :

Answer honestly,

Accept my partners' answers,

Have a great time,

Love, live and laugh,

Not to be shy.

Signed by
_____
And
_____

Table of content:

Introduction to the book_____4

How to use this book_____5

Questions regarding:

    Love and everything else in our relationship_____6
    Personal thoughts_____21
    Do you Even know me that well !_____23
    Personal thoughts_____35
    Who is most likely to ... ?_____37
    Personal thoughts_____52
    You, me and what about The rest of the World? _____54
    Personal thoughts_____73
    The Hot or Not Questions_____75
    Personal thoughts_____91

Final thoughts_____93

Introduction

In every relationship, we face ups and downs, moments of joy and moments of sadness yet, we are always searching for happiness and constantly wanting to make our partner happier and we consider this to be our ultimate goal! But the real difficulty is not how to make each other more cheerful but how can we as a couple grow together in the SAME RIGHT direction?

Sharing moments of fun, joy and laughter is key for keeping a great connection with your lover, however, in order for you to grow in the same right direction you will have to open up to each other, communicate about everything in your lives, be as transparent as possible and as understanding as you can be. This journal will help you connect with your partner in a completely new level, no matter what stage of a relationship you are in, you will discover your partner's thoughts and feelings in a deeper and honest way; you will also rediscover your partners' favorite things in life, because over time meaningful and fun conversations tend to decrease. In this book, you will have cultivating conversations, explore your oldest and newest memories, reset your values, and learn how to create a fulfilling life together just by answering some questions that are sometimes intimate and deep and other times fun and hot!

By Elodie Garner

How to use this book

This Journal has five sections, each aiming to make you closer to each other. You can start with the section of your preference, you can respect the order of questions or mix them up.

If you and your partner live in the same house you can consider this as an activity to do together every day (answering as many questions as you would like). Taking notes of your answers is a great thing to do, because you can go back to this journal after years go by, and remember how you and your partner felt about certain things, and you can do this activity again and compare how you evolved together.

If you live apart from each other, you can have a journal for yourself and provide one for your partner, each one of you will answer her or his questions and you can interchange your journals to discover how your lover feels and thinks about different topics.

Love and everything else in our relationship

This category of questions aims to help you discover your partner in a deepest way, understand each other better, learn more about each other's pasts. Here, you will find questions about your personalities, your feelings and emotions, your past (some secrets maybe!) and all the things you enjoy and dislike about life and each other.

Love and Everything else in our relationship

Do you remember when we first met? Where was it? And what was I wearing? *You better remember everything* ☺

Partner A:

_____

_____

_____

Partner B:

_____

_____

What was your first impression about me? Did it change over time?

Partner A:

_____

_____

_____

Partner B:

_____

_____

7

Love and Everything else in our relationship

When we met, did you ever imagine that our relationship will go this far? And why or why not?

Partner A:

_____

_____

_____

_____

Partner B:

_____

_____

_____

Here, draw the Emoji that describes the best your emotion when we met:

Partner A:

Day 1   Day 2   Day 3

◯   ◯   ◯

Partner B:

Day 1   Day 2   Day 3

◯   ◯   ◯

Love and Everything else in our relationship

What is your favorite memory of dating me?

Partner A:

_____

_____

_____

_____

Partner B:

_____

_____

_____

Do you believe that behind our love and relationship a superpower (God, Faith...) exists? Or was it just random luck ?

Partner A:

_____

_____

_____

_____

Partner B:

_____

_____

_____

9

Love and Everything else in our relationship

What did you enjoy the most about our first date ?

Partner A:

_____

_____

_____

_____

Partner B:

_____

_____

_____

What did you worry about the most in our first date ?

Partner A:

_____

_____

_____

_____

Partner B:

_____

_____

_____

Love and Everything else in our relationship

Back then, what did you consider was the most attracting feature about my personality ? Did you change your mind about it ?

Partner A:

_____

_____

_____

_____

Partner B:

_____

_____

_____

What did you consider was the most attracting physical thing about me? Did you change your mind about it ?

Partner A:

_____

_____

_____

Partner B:

_____

_____

_____

Love and Everything else in our relationship

When did you realize that you have feelings for me ? Do you still feel the same way?

Partner A:

_____
_____
_____
_____

Partner B:

_____
_____
_____

When expressing how you feel for me, what was your biggest fear? What is the reaction you expected from me?

Partner A:

_____
_____
_____
_____

Partner B:

_____
_____
_____

Love and Everything else in our relationship

If you go back in time would you change something about our first days together?

Partner A:

_____

_____

_____

Partner B:

_____

_____

_____

Did you ever had a doubt about my personality, my story ... ? What was it?

Partner A:

_____

_____

_____

Partner B:

_____

_____

_____

Love and Everything else in our relationship

At that time, did you have any deal-breakers or things that would make you seriously reconsider our relationship?

Partner A:

_____

_____

_____

_____

Partner B:

_____

_____

_____

What's one secret you've wanted to tell me back then, but haven't?

Partner A:

_____

_____

_____

_____

Partner B:

_____

_____

_____

Love and Everything else in our relationship

What does love mean to you?

Partner A:

_____

_____

_____

_____

Partner B:

_____

_____

_____

If you had one sentence to describe our relationship what would it be?

Partner A:

_____

_____

_____

Partner B:

_____

_____

_____

15

Love and Everything else in our relationship

What about my personality makes you really happy?

Partner A:

_____

_____

_____

Partner B:

_____

_____

_____

What do you think was the most vulnerable moment in our relationship? How did you feel about it?

Partner A:

_____

_____

_____

Partner B:

_____

_____

_____

Love and Everything else in our relationship

What's one thing you want to do together that we've never done before?

Partner A:

_____
_____
_____

Partner B:

_____
_____
_____

Where is your favorite place to be with me?

Partner A:

_____
_____
_____

Partner B:

_____
_____
_____

Love and Everything else in our relationship

Which one of the following do you think creates the most conflicts in a couple: Money problems, lack of communication, sexual dysfunction or lack of trust?

Partner A:

_____

_____

_____

_____

Partner B:

_____

_____

_____

What do you think is the one thing our relationship is lacking? How would you introduce it?

Partner A:

_____

_____

_____

_____

Partner B:

_____

_____

_____

Love and Everything else in our relationship

What's one similarity between us that you absolutely love?

Partner A:

_____

_____

_____

Partner B:

_____

_____

_____

What's one difference between us that you dislike?

Partner A:

_____

_____

_____

Partner B:

_____

_____

_____

Love and Everything else in our relationship

What's your biggest fear for our relationship right now ?

Partner A:

_____

_____

_____

Partner B:

_____

_____

_____

What physical and emotional gestures do you appreciate most about me ?

Partner A:

_____

_____

_____

Partner B:

_____

_____

_____

Thoughts

Partner A:

Thoughts

Partner B:

_____
_____
_____
_____
_____
_____
_____
_____
_____
_____
_____
_____
_____
_____
_____
_____
_____
_____
_____
_____
_____
_____
_____
_____
_____

Do you Even know me that well !

This category will help you get more intimacy with your partner, over time, we forget to ask our lover about her/his favorite things in life (favorite memories, activities...), her/his feelings about certain situations moreover, fun conversation tend to decrease that is why playing this activity together will reconnect you in a deeper level. These questions will allow you to rediscover your partner's process of thinking and feeling.

Do you even know me that well ?

What is my favorite childhood memory ?

Partner A:

_____

_____

_____

Partner B:

_____

_____

_____

What was my favorite memory of our relationship?

Partner A:

_____

_____

_____

Partner B:

_____

_____

Do you even know me that well ?

What is my favorite song, who is my favorite singer and what is my favorite Movie/TV show ?

Partner A:

Partner B:

What is my favorite activity to do when i am alone?

Partner A:

Partner B:

Do you even know me that well ?

What historical era would I most, and least, want to go to?

Partner A:

Partner B:

Who is my favorite couple in pop culture?

Partner A:

Partner B:

Do you even know me that well ?

What song reminds me of you?

Partner A:

_____

_____

_____

Partner B:

_____

_____

_____

What's the strangest thing I've ever eaten?

Partner A:

_____

_____

_____

Partner B:

_____

_____

_____

Do you even know me that well ?

On a scale of 1 to 10 how jalous do you think I am? How does it make you feel?

Partner A:

_____

_____

Partner B:

_____

_____

Who is the one friend that i trust the most for keeping my secrets? What do you think about him/her?

Partner A:

_____

_____

_____

Partner B:

_____

_____

Do you even know me that well ?

Do you think that i hide a secret that i have never told anyone about, including you? *Oh really you are that innocent!*

Partner A:

_____

_____

_____

Partner B:

_____

_____

_____

Do you think that I consider myself an old soul? Why?

Partner A:

_____

_____

_____

Partner B:

_____

_____

_____

Do you even know me that well ?

What is the most precious object i own?

Partner A:

_____

_____

_____

Partner B:

_____

_____

_____

Which movie do I most regret wasting two hours of my life on?

Partner A:

_____

_____

_____

Partner B:

_____

_____

_____

Do you even know me that well ?

If only one wish could come true what would mine be?

Partner A:

Partner B:

What would constitute a perfect day for me?

Partner A:

Partner B:

Do you even know me that well ?

What are three things on my bucket list?

Partner A:

_____

_____

_____

Partner B:

_____

_____

What's a word or phrase people use that I just can't stand?

Partner A:

_____

_____

_____

Partner B:

_____

_____

Do you even know me that well ?

What are the dreams that i want to reach?

Partner A:

_____

_____

_____

Partner B:

_____

_____

_____

What are the deepest fears that I have?

Partner A:

_____

_____

_____

Partner B:

_____

_____

_____

Do you even know me that well ?

What would I do if I won $10,000?

Partner A:

_____

_____

_____

_____

Partner B:

_____

_____

_____

If you could meet any band, past or present, which one would it be?

Partner A:

_____

_____

_____

_____

Partner B:

_____

_____

_____

 # Thoughts

Partner A:

_____
_____
_____
_____
_____
_____
_____
_____
_____
_____
_____
_____
_____
_____
_____
_____
_____
_____
_____
_____
_____
_____
_____
_____
_____
_____
_____

Thoughts

Partner B:

_____
_____
_____
_____
_____
_____
_____
_____
_____
_____
_____
_____
_____
_____
_____
_____
_____
_____
_____
_____
_____
_____
_____
_____
_____
_____
_____

Who is most likely to...?

This is the perfect game for couples, this category of questions is mostly for fun and laughter, but it is also considered a bonding game for partners. You can play this game with another couple, with friends or in any fun gathering.

Who is most likely to ...?

Who is the best listener?

Partner A:

Definitely me

No doubt, it's You

Partner B:

Definitely me

No doubt, it's You

Who is the best kisser?

Partner A:

Definitely me

No doubt, it's You

Partner B:

Definitely me

No doubt, it's You

Who farts more?

Partner A:

Definitely me

No doubt, it's You

Partner B:

Definitely me

No doubt, it's You

Who is most likely to ...?

Who is a better dancer?

Partner A:

| Definitely me | |
| No doubt, it's You | |

Partner B:

| Definitely me | |
| No doubt, it's You | |

Who loves his parents more?

Partner A:

| Definitely me | |
| No doubt, it's You | |

Partner B:

| Definitely me | |
| No doubt, it's You | |

Who is more forgiving?

Partner A:

| Definitely me | |
| No doubt, it's You | |

Partner B:

| Definitely me | |
| No doubt, it's You | |

Who is most likely to ...?

Who will be (or is) a better parent?

Partner A:

Definitely me

No doubt, it's You

Partner B:

Definitely me

No doubt, it's You

Who is more optimistic?

Partner A:

Definitely me

No doubt, it's You

Partner B:

Definitely me

No doubt, it's You

Who is better looking?

Partner A:

Definitely me

No doubt, it's You

Partner B:

Definitely me

No doubt, it's You

Who is most likely to ...?

Who is a hardworker?

Partner A:

Definitely me	
No doubt, it's You	

Partner B:

Definitely me	
No doubt, it's You	

Who is funnier ?

Partner A:

Definitely me	
No doubt, it's You	

Partner B:

Definitely me	
No doubt, it's You	

Who gives better massages?

Partner A:

Definitely me	
No doubt, it's You	

Partner B:

Definitely me	
No doubt, it's You	

Who is most likely to ...?

Who is better at planning surprises?

Partner A:

Definitely me

No doubt, it's You

Partner B:

Definitely me

No doubt, it's You

Who is a better bathroom singer?

Partner A:

Definitely me

No doubt, it's You

Partner B:

Definitely me

No doubt, it's You

Who lies the most?

Partner A:

Definitely me

No doubt, it's You

Partner B:

Definitely me

No doubt, it's You

Who is most likely to ...?

Who is the smartest?

Partner A:

| Definitely me |
| No doubt, it's You |

Partner B:

| Definitely me |
| No doubt, it's You |

Who drives better?

Partner A:

| Definitely me |
| No doubt, it's You |

Partner B:

| Definitely me |
| No doubt, it's You |

Who gives better advice?

Partner A:

| Definitely me |
| No doubt, it's You |

Partner B:

| Definitely me |
| No doubt, it's You |

Who is most likely to ...?

Who is most likely to forget an anniversary?

Partner A:

Definitely me

No doubt, it's You

Partner B:

Definitely me

No doubt, it's You

Who is most likely to cheat?

Partner A:

Definitely me

No doubt, it's You

Partner B:

Definitely me

No doubt, it's You

Who is most likely to send a dirty text to the wrong person?

Partner A:

Definitely me

No doubt, it's You

Partner B:

Definitely me

No doubt, it's You

Who is most likely to ...?

Who is most likely to crack under pressure?

Partner A:

| Definitely me |
| No doubt, it's You |

Partner B:

| Definitely me |
| No doubt, it's You |

Who is most likely to earn more money?

Partner A:

| Definitely me |
| No doubt, it's You |

Partner B:

| Definitely me |
| No doubt, it's You |

Who is most likely to write a love song?

Partner A:

| Definitely me |
| No doubt, it's You |

Partner B:

| Definitely me |
| No doubt, it's You |

Who is most likely to ...?

Who is most likely to start a fight?

Partner A:

Definitely me

No doubt, it's You

Partner B:

Definitely me

No doubt, it's You

Who is most likely to fall asleep during a movie?

Partner A:

Definitely me

No doubt, it's You

Partner B:

Definitely me

No doubt, it's You

Who is most likely to buy useless stuff?

Partner A:

Definitely me

No doubt, it's You

Partner B:

Definitely me

No doubt, it's You

Who is most likely to ...?

Who is most likely to drop their phone in the toilet?

Partner A:

Definitely me

No doubt, it's You

Partner B:

Definitely me

No doubt, it's You

Who is most likely to win the lottery?

Partner A:

Definitely me

No doubt, it's You

Partner B:

Definitely me

No doubt, it's You

Who is most likely to start an own business?

Partner A:

Definitely me

No doubt, it's You

Partner B:

Definitely me

No doubt, it's You

Who is most likely to ...?

Who is most likely to fall asleep in public?

Partner A:

Definitely me

No doubt, it's You

Partner B:

Definitely me

No doubt, it's You

Who is most likely to want sexting?

Partner A:

Definitely me

No doubt, it's You

Partner B:

Definitely me

No doubt, it's You

Who is most likely to know the names of all the famous pornstars?

Partner A:

Definitely me

No doubt, it's You

Partner B:

Definitely me

No doubt, it's You

Who is most likely to ...?

Who is most likely to flirt by using dirty jokes?

Partner A:

| Definitely me | |
| No doubt, it's You | |

Partner B:

| Definitely me | |
| No doubt, it's You | |

Who is most likely to laugh during a funeral?

Partner A:

| Definitely me | |
| No doubt, it's You | |

Partner B:

| Definitely me | |
| No doubt, it's You | |

Who is most likely to fake an orgasm?

Partner A:

| Definitely me | |
| No doubt, it's You | |

Partner B:

| Definitely me | |
| No doubt, it's You | |

Who is most likely to ...?

Who is most likely to start a YouTube channel?

Partner A:

Definitely me

No doubt, it's You

Partner B:

Definitely me

No doubt, it's You

Who is most likely to act like they're drunk when they're still sober?

Partner A:

Definitely me

No doubt, it's You

Partner B:

Definitely me

No doubt, it's You

Who is most likely to forget to shower?

Partner A:

Definitely me

No doubt, it's You

Partner B:

Definitely me

No doubt, it's You

Who is most likely to ...?

Who is most likely to be a terrible vice president?

Partner A:

Definitely me

No doubt, it's You

Partner B:

Definitely me

No doubt, it's You

Who is most likely to fake it until they make it?

Partner A:

Definitely me

No doubt, it's You

Partner B:

Definitely me

No doubt, it's You

Who is most likely to stay in bed all day?

Partner A:

Definitely me

No doubt, it's You

Partner B:

Definitely me

No doubt, it's You

Thoughts

Partner A:

_____
_____
_____
_____
_____
_____
_____
_____
_____
_____
_____
_____
_____
_____
_____
_____
_____
_____
_____
_____
_____
_____
_____

Thoughts

Partner B:

_____
_____
_____
_____
_____
_____
_____
_____
_____
_____
_____
_____
_____
_____
_____
_____
_____
_____
_____
_____
_____
_____
_____
_____

You, Me... and what about The rest of the World?

In this section, you will share with each other - in an honest- way how you feel about the rest of the world (your families, you friends, your kids ...) . You will discuss some serious topics that you probably didn't have the chance to talk about before, you will set your future goals together and by the end of it get closer to each other.

You, Me... and what about the rest of the world?

What was your first impression of my family?

Partner A:

_____

_____

_____

Partner B:

_____

_____

_____

How do you feel now about the members of my family one by one (mother, father, brother, cousins...) ?

Partner A:

_____

_____

_____

Partner B:

_____

_____

_____

You, Me... and what about the rest of the world?

What is your dream house? And what do you think about ours? Any changes you would want to make?

Partner A:

_____

_____

_____

Partner B:

_____

_____

_____

How do you feel about me reconnecting with my Exs (as friends)?

Partner A:

_____

_____

_____

Partner B:

_____

_____

_____

You, Me... and what about the rest of the world?

Who is the sibling you are closest to? Why?

Partner A:

_____

_____

_____

Partner B:

_____

_____

_____

Who is the black sheep in your family?

Partner A:

_____

_____

_____

Partner B:

_____

_____

_____

You, Me... and what about the rest of the world?

What is the thing you most appreciate about your parents?

Partner A:
_____
_____
_____

Partner B:
_____
_____
_____

Do you have a difficult time setting limits with your family?

Partner A:
_____
_____
_____

Partner B:
_____
_____
_____

You, Me... and what about the rest of the world?

Is there anything with your family that may impact your relationship with me?

Partner A:

_____

_____

_____

_____

Partner B:

_____

_____

_____

How have family members reacted to your previous relationships?

Partner A:

_____

_____

_____

_____

Partner B:

_____

_____

_____

You, Me... and what about the rest of the world?

Who would you say is the most unusual of my family members that you have met?

Partner A:

_____

_____

_____

Partner B:

_____

_____

_____

How important is it to you that you and your partner be on good terms with each other's families?

Partner A:

_____

_____

_____

Partner B:

_____

_____

You, Me... and what about the rest of the world?

What is something your parents did or used to do that really embarrassed you?

Partner A:

_____

_____

_____

Partner B:

_____

_____

_____

What is the best or worst thing you inherited from your parents?

Partner A:

_____

_____

_____

Partner B:

_____

_____

You, Me... and what about the rest of the world?

What petty thing that people do really gets on your nerves?

Partner A:

_____

_____

_____

Partner B:

_____

_____

_____

Describe what it was like for you when your parents were angry with each other?

Partner A:

_____

_____

_____

Partner B:

_____

_____

_____

You, Me... and what about the rest of the world?

Who is one couple that you admire? What is it that makes this couple's relationship great?

Partner A:

_____

_____

_____

Partner B:

_____

_____

_____

Describe the type of family culture that you would ideally like to have.

Partner A:

_____

_____

_____

Partner B:

_____

_____

_____

You, Me... and what about the rest of the world?

What is one thing that your parents did right in raising you? Why was this so meaningful?

Partner A:

_____

_____

_____

Partner B:

_____

_____

_____

What do you think are the most important things parents can do to raise great kids?

Partner A:

_____

_____

_____

Partner B:

_____

_____

_____

You, Me... and what about the rest of the world?

What do you consider the most important qualities of a lasting friendship?

Partner A:

_____

_____

_____

Partner B:

_____

_____

How would you describe your role in your family now that you are an adult? Do you think your role has changed?

Partner A:

_____

_____

_____

Partner B:

_____

_____

You, Me... and what about the rest of the world?

Do you think I am a lot like the other members of my family? How am I like them?

Partner A:

Partner B:

Do you like it when friends feel comfortable enough to drop by unexpectedly?

Partner A:

Partner B:

You, Me... and what about the rest of the world?

On a typical day/night out with your friends, what do you do?

Partner A:

_____

_____

_____

Partner B:

_____

_____

_____

Do any of your friends have things that make you envious?

Partner A:

_____

_____

_____

Partner B:

_____

_____

_____

You, Me... and what about the rest of the world?

Which of your friends is most successful? Would you like to have the same level of success?

Partner A:

Partner B:

Do you think you are a good influence on your friends?

Partner A:

Partner B:

You, Me... and what about the rest of the world?

Do you think we should spend holidays with certain family members or would you like to spend holidays alone (and with any kids we might have) for a change?

Partner A:

_____

_____

_____

Partner B:

_____

_____

_____

At this stage in your life do you think you would prefer having children or being child-free? Do you think your feeling might change?

Partner A:

_____

_____

_____

Partner B:

_____

_____

_____

You, Me... and what about the rest of the world?

Do you have any strong preferences on naming our children?

Partner A:

_____

_____

_____

Partner B:

_____

_____

_____

Should we try to move to an area that has a really good school system for our children?

Partner A:

_____

_____

_____

Partner B:

_____

_____

You, Me... and what about the rest of the world?

Do you think we should have kids (or another kid) in the short term?

Partner A:
_____
_____
_____
_____

Partner B:
_____
_____
_____

Do you think that i manage my time well between work family the house....?

Partner A:
_____
_____
_____
_____

Partner B:
_____
_____
_____

You, Me... and what about the rest of the world?

How do you see our future together 5 years from now?

Partner A:
_____
_____
_____

Partner B:
_____
_____
_____

What are your professional plans for the future?

Partner A:
_____
_____
_____

Partner B:
_____
_____
_____

Thoughts

Partner A:

_____

_____

_____

_____

_____

_____

_____

_____

_____

_____

_____

_____

_____

_____

_____

_____

_____

_____

_____

_____

_____

_____

_____

 # Thoughts

Partner B:

_____

_____

_____

_____

_____

_____

_____

_____

_____

_____

_____

_____

_____

_____

_____

_____

_____

_____

_____

_____

_____

_____

_____

_____

_____

_____

_____

_____

The Hot or Not Questions

In this section, you will share with each other your opinions about sex in general and your sexual life in particular. This game will help you get more intimate with your partner and strengthen your bonds.

The Hot or Not Questions

Do you have a preference between sex in the morning or at night?

Partner A:
_____
_____
_____

Partner B:
_____
_____
_____

Are there times when you just want a "quickie"? When are those?

Partner A:
_____
_____
_____

Partner B:
_____
_____

The Hot or Not Questions

Do you like talking dirty sex ?

Partner A:

Partner B:

What do I do that gives you the most sexual pleasure?

Partner A:

Partner B:

The Hot or Not Questions

Are you satisfied with our sexual life?

Partner A:

Partner B:

Do you think we should try new methods in bed?

Partner A:

Partner B:

The Hot or Not Questions

Do you ever feel bored when we have sex ?

Partner A:

_____

_____

_____

_____

Partner B:

_____

_____

_____

Do you ever feel pressure when i ask you if you want to have sex?

Partner A:

_____

_____

_____

_____

Partner B:

_____

_____

_____

The Hot or Not Questions

How did you feel about the first time we had propre sex?

Partner A:

_____

_____

_____

Partner B:

_____

_____

_____

Do you enjoy having sex with me less or more than before? And why?

Partner A:

_____

_____

_____

Partner B:

_____

_____

_____

The Hot or Not Questions

What was your very first orgasm like?

Partner A:

_____

_____

_____

Partner B:

_____

_____

_____

Have you ever had wet dreams while you were with me?

Partner A:

_____

_____

_____

Partner B:

_____

_____

_____

The Hot or Not Questions

How important do you think sex is in a relationship?

Partner A:

_____

_____

_____

_____

Partner B:

_____

_____

_____

Have you ever did something related to sex that you feel ashamed about? What is it?

Partner A:

_____

_____

_____

_____

Partner B:

_____

_____

_____

The Hot or Not Questions

What is the one thing that you love the most about our sexual relationship?

Partner A:
_____
_____
_____
_____

Partner B:
_____
_____
_____

Do you think that sexual dysfunction is a propre reason for a person to cheat on his or her partner? Why? Why not?

Partner A:
_____
_____
_____

Partner B:
_____
_____
_____

The Hot or Not Questions

Have you ever thought about cheating on me?

Partner A:

Partner B:

Do you believe that sex is as important as love?

Partner A:

Partner B:

The Hot or Not Questions

Do you feel that our sexual relationship is getting better? Why?

Partner A:

_____

_____

_____

Partner B:

_____

_____

_____

What is your deepest sexual fantasy ?

Partner A:

_____

_____

_____

Partner B:

_____

_____

_____

The Hot or Not Questions

Have you ever faked an orgasm?

Partner A:

_____

_____

_____

Partner B:

_____

_____

_____

How do you define great sex?

Partner A:

_____

_____

_____

Partner B:

_____

_____

_____

The Hot or Not Questions

Does the thought of someone watching us having sex excite you?

Partner A:

_____

_____

_____

_____

Partner B:

_____

_____

_____

Is there a type of outfit or clothes you find sexy that you'd like to see me in?

Partner A:

_____

_____

_____

Partner B:

_____

_____

_____

The Hot or Not Questions

Do you like playing with sex toys, or would you like to try them as a couple?

Partner A:

_____

_____

_____

Partner B:

_____

_____

_____

What's something not obviously sexual that turns you on?

Partner A:

_____

_____

_____

Partner B:

_____

_____

_____

The Hot or Not Questions

Do you feel that you have a sexual dysfunction?

Partner A:

_____

_____

_____

_____

Partner B:

_____

_____

_____

Do you think that couples should consider visiting a sexual therapist?

Partner A:

_____

_____

_____

Partner B:

_____

_____

_____

The Hot or Not Questions

Is there anything about your body that affects your sexuality?

Partner A:

Partner B:

Do you like to be in control in bed? Why?

Partner A:

Partner B:

Thoughts

Partner A:

_____
_____
_____
_____
_____
_____
_____
_____
_____
_____
_____
_____
_____
_____
_____
_____
_____
_____
_____
_____
_____
_____
_____
_____
_____
_____

 # Thoughts

Partner B:

_____

_____

_____

_____

_____

_____

_____

_____

_____

_____

_____

_____

_____

_____

_____

_____

_____

_____

_____

_____

_____

_____

_____

_____

_____

_____

_____

_____

Final Thoughts

In this section, you will feel free to write your feelings and thoughts about things you have learned about your partner. You can describe and share with eachother how you feel or even write letters to one another and you could add in this section new questions that you want to ask your lover!

 # Final Thoughts

Partner A:

_____

_____

_____

_____

_____

_____

_____

_____

_____

_____

_____

_____

_____

_____

_____

_____

_____

_____

_____

_____

_____

_____

_____

_____

 # Final Thoughts

Partner A:

_____
_____
_____
_____
_____
_____
_____
_____
_____
_____
_____
_____
_____
_____
_____
_____
_____
_____
_____
_____
_____
_____
_____

 # Final Thoughts

Partner A:

_____
_____
_____
_____
_____
_____
_____
_____
_____
_____
_____
_____
_____
_____
_____
_____
_____
_____
_____
_____
_____
_____
_____
_____

 # Final Thoughts

Partner B:

_____

_____

_____

_____

_____

_____

_____

_____

_____

_____

_____

_____

_____

_____

_____

_____

_____

_____

_____

_____

_____

 # Final Thoughts

Partner B:

_____
_____
_____
_____
_____
_____
_____
_____
_____
_____
_____
_____
_____
_____
_____
_____
_____
_____
_____
_____
_____
_____
_____
_____
_____
_____
_____
_____

 # Final Thoughts

Partner B:

_____
_____
_____
_____
_____
_____
_____
_____
_____
_____
_____
_____
_____
_____
_____
_____
_____
_____
_____
_____
_____
_____
_____
_____
_____
_____

Made in the USA
Coppell, TX
08 December 2024

41999778R00056